# REFLECTIONS ON LIF[E]
## Birth to Death

*Raymond S. Nelson*

Winston-Derek Publishers, Inc.
Pennywell Drive—Post Office Box 90883
Nashville, Tennessee 37209

## Contents

| | |
|---|---|
| At Birth | 1 |
| New Life | 2 |
| Mark Andrew | 3 |
| First Step | 5 |
| All Things New | 6 |
| Trust | 7 |
| Kindergarten | 8 |
| The Climbing Tree | 9 |
| Know Thyself | 10 |
| Rite of Passage | 11 |
| Courtship | 13 |
| Peerless | 14 |
| Mantrap | 15 |
| My Margaret | 16 |
| Heaven or Hell | 17 |
| Marriage | 18 |
| I Take You | 19 |
| Anno Domini, 1996 | 20 |
| Constancy | 21 |
| Love | 22 |
| When I Consider | 23 |
| My Daughter | 25 |
| My Son | 26 |
| Parting | 27 |
| Healing Touch | 29 |
| Life's Lottery | 31 |
| The Merry Go Round | 32 |
| Out of the Depths | 33 |
| In a Far Country | 34 |

| | |
|---|---|
| Yet Will I Trust | 35 |
| Self Sacrifice | 36 |
| Simplicity | 37 |
| Distant Goal | 39 |
| At Symphony | 41 |
| Relationships | 42 |
| Gift of God | 43 |
| Or I Die | 44 |
| Family Treasures | 45 |
| Memories | 46 |
| Drouth | 47 |
| Retirement | 48 |
| Two at Eighty | 49 |
| John Michener | 50 |
| Dialogue | 51 |
| Active Aging | 52 |
| Wheels Within Wheels | 53 |
| Life Runs Out | 54 |
| Ending Is Beginning | 55 |
| Heartbeat | 56 |
| Betrayal | 57 |
| Composing Stick | 59 |
| Last Rites | 60 |

## *At Birth*

An infant is a glorious dawn,
   A cropland newly tilled,
A vessel launched on unknown seas,
   A promise unfulfilled.

Each dawn must run its course till dusk,
   Each field its harvest yield,
Each vessel find its harbor home,
   Each promise be revealed.

New life is daybreak of an age,
   Is fertile field just sown,
Is voyage on uncharted seas,
   Toward destinies unknown.

## *New Life*

Cocoons and pupae bide their time
Till butterflies appear
To soar as monarchs of the field
In robes beyond compare.

## *Mark Andrew*

Oh Gift of God, oh Child of Grace,
On Thy and our behalf, once more
We gather in this holy place
To offer thanks and God adore.

In spirit and in truth we share
The sacrament, the holy word;
We join in song and simple prayer
In promise that we shall be heard.

We meditate on earlier days
When Mark and Andrew walked the earth
And daily on Christ's face could gaze,
As we cannot—yet in your birth

(A mystery unplumbed, unknown)
The future spreads before our eyes,
The promise of an age to come,
New rainbow in these clouded skies.

Oh Son of God, though Child of Earth,
We consecrate ourselves, and you,
To seek these things of greatest worth
In confidence that God is true.


(Bulletin insert at the baptism of Mark Andrew Nelson, March 1979, in First Covenant Church, Sioux City, Iowa.)

Henry Vaughan wrote three memorable lines in his poem "The World" (1655) which are unforgettable to me. The lines are breathtaking in their audacity and vision:
> I saw eternity the other night
> Like a great ring of pure and endless light,
> All calm as it was bright.

In the poem Vaughan sees a steady radiance and underneath it the Ptolemaic cosmos, with its concentric spheres and, at its center, feverish human activity.

When I first learned by telephone that my namesake had taken his first steps, I thought of Vaughan's lines. Only one halting step, to be sure, but just think of what it meant. That child in his first step gave promise of unimaginable motion. He may in his lifetime engage in interplanetary travel. He will certainly walk thousands of miles. Clearly, that one short step held promise of an incalculable future, and that's part of the wonder of unfolding life.

## *First Step*

We annihilated space today.
Distance crumbled into nothingness,
While spheres in orbit tumbled into disarray.
But fresh new worlds came into view
As Raymond stepped out all alone
To meet, on sturdy legs, the new.

> (Raymond Stanley Nelson III
> walked in January, 1984.)

## *All Things New*

A youngster greets each sight and sound
   Of daily life and special days
     With shining eyes and fetching ways
In dazzling wonders newly found.

The adolescent plays it cool
   In spite of callow youth, yet grows
     In poise and grace and stature, shows
Rich promise of mature self-rule.

The middle-aged, now rich in pelf—
   In children, houses, crops, and land—
     Take time to search for meaning, and
In God find substance for the self.

The silver-crowned, now up in years,
   Leave their eight-to-fives to learn
     New skills, or crowd the roads, or turn
To busy days as volunteers.

## *Trust*

"Grampa can fix it," the three year old said
As he handed his tractor to me.
"See? It's broken right here,"
And he added a shaft and two wheels.
He was talking to no one particular
—Perhaps to himself—
As he stood at my knee.
I looked at the pieces
And then at his face,
Then back to the wreck in my lap.
"Oh, T. J.," I started, then stopped,
As he tipped back his head.
I looked at his face,
His damp curls and blue eyes,
The confident set of his chin.
I wavered, and knew I must try.
"Why, sure, Little Fellow, let's give it a whirl,"
And I knew I must magic perform.

## *Kindergarten*

Bright-eyed children clambered everywhere
On teeter-totter, swing and slide, while shout
And laughter echoed through the morning air.

They seemed like blossoms with their windblown hair,
Their open faces, and their sturdy frames,
As I watched in pleasure from my playground chair.

## *The Climbing Tree*

Just a pollard now remains. This noon
Two men arrived with ladder, rope, and saw,
And lopped the branches one by one, till soon
The cottonwood, destroyed, now stands in ruin.

The scraggly limbs yet standing show the scars
The boys made as they clambered up the stem.
The platform's there; bent nails still hold the bars
Which cross the limbs, as on a mast the spars.

It was their hideout. There an urgent call
Fell on deaf ears. A sister's plea, a mother's
Scold, a brother's taunt could never pall.
Tomorrow morning they will take it all.

(A pollard is a tree that has had its limbs cut back to the trunk. Years ago I saw such a tree being removed, with remnants of a tree house on its trunk, and I associated it in my imagination with the playhouse our children built high up in a tree in our back yard.)

## *Know Thyself*

You cannot live another's life
   Nor die another's death;
You cannot look through other's eyes
   Nor breathe another's breath.

You yourself must look and breathe
   And live and die alone,
Creating daily what you are
   And what you will become.

## *Rite of Passage*

" . . . Take a left . . . now a right . . . "
Park parallel at that curb . . .
Stop at the crest of the hill, then start . . .
Choose your lane, and drive . . .
    Good.    Good.

"Now, back to the station.
You've done well.
From now on you're on wheels.
You're a driver
    In our world."

Courtship rites are perennially interesting. All Nature Shows on public television attest to the fascination we exhibit in watching ruffed grouse, wild turkeys, quail, partridge, pheasants perform their nuptial ceremonies. All animals and birds have their ways of pairing, some more spectacular than others. Even human beings have their rituals of dating, those complex patterns of behavior that can lead, when all goes well, to matrimony. Who does the choosing is always debatable, though the best evidence suggests that both the man and woman are centrally engaged in deciding whether the match is a good one.

## *Courtship*

He preens his feathers, puffs his chest,
Croons a love song—she's impressed
    (But she plays coy, she looks askance).
    He tries harder, starts to dance,
He whirls and struts and tunes his voice
Until she's taken—he's her choice!

## *Peerless*

Every rose is special, no two are
The same. Petals curl in petals, till blooms
Are fully blown, and fragrant mists float far
Afield to fuse with other spring perfumes.
Each oak tree is different, each one stands
Alone, reaching broadly, reaching tall,
With no two crowns alike. For each commands
Its proper due and place in midst of all.
A man's beloved is peerless, shares her place
With none. Her form, her grace, her poise, her charm
Combine through matchless means to make her face
The symbol of perfection for his arm.
Each rose and oak and woman is unique,
My dear; You are the treasure that I seek.

## *Mantrap*

Jo circled slowly round the laden board
To verify that all things were in place.
She turned her full attention to the lace
And crystal, silverware and plate, but scored
Her triumph in the rosebud blooms which soared
Above the goblets' spiry, slender grace
In unifying strength. The dining space,
She seemed to say, was ready to afford
Him welcome. One quick last glance she threw
Before she set the stereo music low
And lit the twelve-inch tapers, with a view
To being ready when he came, to show
Him warm attentive care in hopes he too
Might find her what he had in mind to know.

## *My Margaret*

The pearl of greatest price is she,
The gem of highest worth,
The diadem which crowns my life
And beautifies the earth!


(The word *pearl* is *marguerite* in French.)

## *Heaven or Hell*

I know where heaven is. It's in your smile,
Your loving presence, all you do and say.
It's in the hours we spend at work and play,
The gentle words which lack pretense and guile.
It's walking hand in hand each patient mile
Or standing side by side at household chore.
It's sharing joy and sorrow, less and more,
In faith and hope that make each day worthwhile.
I know of hell as well. It's in the void,
The echoes sounding through each empty room
Where otherwise your cheery voice would sound
With mine. It's in long tedious hours employed,
Then weary evenings, silent as a tomb.
It's missing you as earth spins round and round.

## *Marriage*

True marriage is a blending of two minds,
Two spirits become one. As oaks are made
More sturdy by the wind, each partner
Grows in strength through gentle pressure
And the shocks of life.

True marriage is a new embodiment,
Male and female sharing bed and board
And bringing forth the fruits of love
As God ordained from immemorial mists
For creatures here below.

True marriage is a giving and receiving,
Two lives that intertwine like vine and elm,
Supporting now, enfolding then, as each
Responds to each in weakness and in strength
While years in cycles roll.

## *"I Take You . . . "*

A man and woman join their lives
For better or for worse
While fully two, they're fully one,
A brand new universe.

   A married pair is one in two,
   The yolk and white restored,
   The yin and yang, the circle squared,
   A whole as halves accord.

      The two who share their deepest love
      Who each in kindness serve,
      Survive the cares and shocks of life
      Nor need from vows to swerve.

## *Anno Domini, 1996*

"And do you take this man?"
"I do."
"Now you may kiss the bride."
So they became a man and wife,
Began the wonder of their wedded life.

"I take you as you are, my dear,
With hopes and dreams and e'en a fear
or two, with strengths and weaknesses
That plague us all," they said.

"We'll round each other out, we'll fill
The gaps, those empty spaces still
within. With patient tenderness
Our years in love we'll tread."

"We'll each have public lives to live,
For work demands its own. We'll give
each other full support, express
Our bond at home, instead."

"We know that storm and struggle come
To every pair. We'll not escape some
tests of health, or need, the stress
That comes on every head."

Thus they spoke their wedding vows,
Lucille and Stan, that wintry day.
A score of years has meantime passed;
Life's better now than e'er, they say.

## *Constancy*

The old-time products, ways of doing things,
Are gone. All things become "improved" or "new,"
And force time-honored ways to take to wings
As upstart ways replace the tried and true.
Nothing's free from change. Our house, once bare,
Now nestles deep within the shrubs and trees
We set as saplings, watered, trimmed with care,
Until our acre should by blooming please.
Our friends, who watched them grow, have through the years
Begun to age and wither, some to fail,
And some to go, till I am left with fears
We too shall weaken, battered by time's flail.
Yet in this steady flux I find you true;
I celebrate the constancy I find in you.

## *Love*

"The more you give, the more you have,"
   She said to John her son,
And spoke, her husband knew full well,
   From wisdom slowly won.

He'd watched her meet the children's needs,
   Mid fretful fevers, health—
Through midnight vigils, morning light—
   In poverty and wealth.

He'd known her constancy to him
   Despite the storms of life,
The daily batterings, the wounds
   She'd dressed as loving wife.

She'd given, given, given—till
   She had no more to give.
But having given all she had
   She'd freed herself to live.

## *When I Consider . . .*

When I consider how my days are spent
In philosophic quest on spongy soil
Or futile sessions mired in precedent,
In jangling strife or ministrative toil;
When I encounter greedy, grasping men
Who mask their avaricious ways in guile,
Or selfish souls whose only regimen
Consists of egocentric ploy or wile;
When I have jounced and bounced on bumpy streets,
And threaded carefully through crowded halls
Beneath an incubus of noise that beats
And throbs until I reach my study walls;
I draw a breath, relax, and think of you,
Restored thereby to face the day anew.

Two ideas form the skeleton of this poem. The first is the Biblical parable of the talents (Matthew 25) which makes clear the principle of stewardship. The servants in the story are entrusted with the master's wealth; it is not their own. Yet they are under obligation to do their best in the investment of the riches that are theirs to use.

The second is the awareness that we do not own our children. Children are unique, separate individuals from the moment of birth. Children are ours, as parents, to nurture, to guide, to teach, to encourage; they never belong to us. And when in the fullness of time they are fully independent of parents and home, the stewardship of parents becomes fully evident in the fruits of their patient, loving care over a score of years.

## *My Daughter*

God loaned an infant child to me,
    A talent to comprise.
She lived with me a score of years
    And proved a precious prize.

She was not chattel, though my charge,
    Not property, but free,
A trust the Lord of Life endowed
    And left consigned to me.

She returned a hundredfold
    Her worth in love and care—
Her steward, I am rich in soul
    From tending one so rare.

## *My Son*

You are my immortality, my son,
And I bequeath my best. Look not to pence
Or sense to guide your steps each day from hence.
God will supply your need. With wisdom won
You'll learn to balance things of heav'n and earth
And thrive as steward of all things of worth
In life, to finish well as you've begun.

## *Parting*

Destined to leave in minutes, I
Clung to my beloved, she to me.
The gate had cleared, the moment neared,
And soon we'd be apart for months.
"I'll write," she said. "And I," I said.
The words came slow, the seconds raced.
"It won't be long till I am home
Again," I said. "I know," she said,
"But home will be so empty while
You're gone." The words fell flat and dull,
As heavily as frost in May.
But as the final call drew near
I said, "My dear, the one moon shines
Both here and there. Let's pledge our faith
That when we see that silver orb
We'll think how we are one in truth
And love, despite the miles between."
A single tear rolled down her cheek
As she looked up, and said, "I will.
Though half a world may lie between,
Our common moon will make us one."

When my youngest son was about twelve years old, I came into the house one afternoon to find him sprawled face down on the frontroom couch, crying bitterly. I quickly knelt at his side and immediately smelled scorched hair. I soon saw his singed lashes, brows, as well as shriveled blond locks of hair. I comforted him by talking softly and gently rubbing his back. The story slowly came out. He had been mimicking his big brothers, trying to make a rocket from black powder and sulphur. But when he lit the rocket in the back yard, the whole thing blew up in his face. He was frightened both in fear for his eyes and face, and in fear of what his parents would say. He needed at that time a reassuring touch and a gentle voice.

The last stanza is based on my memory of a close friend who felt at eighty-two that he'd been cheated in life: he could no longer drive his car or play his mandolin or wander about town as he once had. Instead he sat in his chair reading ads for groceries and other things. He was bitter and aloof, isolated from other persons until the magic of a human touch broke through his loneliness and established rapport once more. One warm human hand said more through its grasp than a thousand words or pictures could ever do.

## *Healing Touch*

A lonely woman, deep in debt
And desperate in her body's need
Seeks help. She sees the Master's face
Yet dares no more than touch his hem—
That's all it takes!

A disobedient child outstretched
In tears, his hair and eyebrows singed,
His features burned, finds healing peace,
Forgiveness, in his father's arms,
And loving care.

A teenage rebel storms upstairs
In hopeless, speechless rage. But soon
A gentle knock, a "Don't come in . . .
Come in." Then tears, a gentle touch,
And healing words.

A couple wander aimlessly
Within the maze of modern life
Till cancer strikes, and chaos reigns.
But they embrace, repledge their faith,
And overcome.

An aged man sits bolt upright
And stiff in his recliner chair
Remote from wife, from us, from all
Until I press his hand in love:
He presses back!

Raoul Wallenberg is a Swede who saved the lives of 100,000 Hungarian Jews the last months of World War II. He was, however, subsequently imprisoned by the Russians as a spy, and, as far as we know, remains buried alive in the Russian gulag. How can a good man suffer such undeserved suffering? And has Wallenberg not surely prayed to God for deliverance, wondering why? Things have happened to him as they have, much as Job insistently challenged God in his day to make clear why he was suffering. The suffering of the righteous continues to be a dilemma in the life of God's people.

Job wondered not only about his own case, but also about his fellows who seemed to be suffering undeservedly. He writes, "From out of the city the dying groan, and the soul of the wounded cries for help; yet God pays no attention to their prayers." (Job 24)

## *Life's Lottery*

The wheel of fortune spins both good and bad
To all alike. There are no favorites.
Saint and sinner live through jars and joys
Each day and hour. From Job to Wallenberg
The story is the same. Good men—God's men
And women—often lose their bets when black
Comes up instead of red, and hail or drouth
Destroys a summer's work . . . or cancer strikes . . .
Or unemployment . . . death of a spouse or child . . .
When drunken drivers slaughter innocents,
Or drug-crazed minors terrorize a town.
It might as well have been rich grain-filled bins,
Trim sun-tanned bodies, thriving crowded hearths,
Clean peaceful streets and happy schools.
It might as well have been a world at peace
Where truth and goodness really do prevail,
And justice reigns for poor as well as rich.
The lots of life fall as they will, and men
And women win or lose the game each day.
Does wisdom come through suffering? Is God
The god of good and not of ill? Does faith
Prepare men's hearts and minds to take the shocks
In stride when joys dissolve in want and tears?
Will "sovereignty" suffice? Can I with Job
Declare "Thy will is mine," and fret no more
For loss and pain quite undeserved? Can I
In patience suffer prison, punishment
And death while God seems silent and aloof?
I do not know. I only know that love
Is best, and love in action is the way
To peace on earth, for strength to meet the quirks
Of chance that force themselves on us each day.

## *The Merry Go Round*

John and Susan climbed aboard
The gilded frame that whirled them round
As loud bells clanged and tall pipes roared
A raucous hurdy-gurdy sound.

They hurtled on a pitching steed,
They later rode a stately swan,
They stood at times, they sat at need,
And whirled and spun and circled on.

They saw blurred faces rushing by,
They glimpsed a thousand flickering lights,
They rode and chased with glittering eye
A host of insubstantial sights.

They're on a carousel which turns,
Which moves and moves, but can't arrive;
They're doomed to spin, unless each learns
They must step off to come alive.

## *Out of the Depths*

Valleys rise to mountaintops
Yet bed the living streams that glide—
The springs and pools and brooks that flow—
Between the heights on either side.

Sorrows soar, in time, to joy
As healing balms pervade the soul,
Drawn from wells the Spirit fills
To help make wounded beings whole.


"There is nothing so sad in life as a wasted sorrow."
Elfrida Foulds

## *In a Far Country*

The jostling women crowd the shops
To buy their vegetables and rice
And fish, ignoring vendors' cries
And roar of buses, trams, and cars.

I watch them haggle prices, make
A choice, then hurry home to man
And household, leaving me behind
To think of you so far away.

## *Yet Will I Trust*

Out of the silence nothing comes
As I wait and listen and wait
Wondering, worrying, puzzled, and down,
I listen, I listen, and wait.

The still small voice says nothing to me
Though I pray and listen and wait,
"Oh God, you know I believe, but why
Are you silent? Why must I wait?

My questions engulf me, my doubts overwhelm,
Why don't you answer, Oh Lord?"
My importunate cry, I raise in my prayer,
As in silence I listen and wait.

"Where is the answer, where is your voice,
Our God, our Sustainer, our Help?"
The enemy threatens, my soul is borne down,
As I wonder and listen and wait.

Your grace is my portion, your strength is my shield,
So I patiently listen and wait.
I quiet my thoughts, I manage my mind,
While I listen in silence. And wait.

    Men ought always to pray, and not to faint.
                                                         Luke 18:1

## *Self Sacrifice*

Some say to me that self is sin,
That moral duty must begin
With simple self-denial in
The service of man's kith and kin.
Such thinking is quite clearly thin,
For I observe beneath the skin
Of every man, his self, my twin:
The service of the self is sin,
It seems, only when the self's within.


> "Love of one's neighbor is not possible without love of oneself."
> Herman Hesse
> *Steppenwolf,* p. 11

## *Simplicity*

The joys of life reside in simple things:
In cooling breezes, summer sun, in air
That hints of rain, in apples, cherries, pears
Picked ripe, and mountain streams, and crooked pines.
I revel in a sunset, mists that crown
A peak, in endless fields of waving grain,
In wooded hills, and rivers flowing free.
I cherish smiles and kindly words, a hand-
Clasp and warm comradeship, the strength of age,
The glow of youth, and childhood's trusting ways.

I spent two months one summer as an exchange professor in Korea. During that time I hiked many miles, seeing the country and learning about its culture. I visited several Buddhist shrines and temples, often climbing to great heights and remote places to get to them. The shrines were typically in out-of-the-way places because inaccessibility offered a measure of safety during those times that Buddhism was out of favor. I remember one shrine in particular that a friend and I labored to reach. The path was narrow, steep, and rough. I clambered over rocks and roots, often pulling myself upward with the help of saplings and trees. My leg muscles quivered from fatigue. But the lure of that historic shrine kept us going despite the difficulties and our weariness, and we reached our goal.

## *Distant Goal*

The mountain path still spiraled up
As I climbed slowly, breathing hard,
The lure an ancient Buddhist shrine
Remote from city, field, and throng.

I pressed ahead on beaten ground
Up rocks and roots, on stepping stones;
I circled trees and mountain streams,
Weary, winded, almost spent.

Yet thought of sacred mountain cave
Where Wonhyo one time lived and wrote
(In Silla's day) kept me on course
Those final grueling, aching steps.

> (Wonhyo was an exemplary Buddhist monk during the Silla dynasty in Korea.)

Symphonies and long poems are alike in that there are sometimes moments of genius along the way. Within rather ordinary stretches of harmony, brief passages can emerge that are brilliant and breathtaking. The tenor solo in Nicolai's *Merry Wives of Windsor,* or a brief melody in Berlioz's *Symphonie Fantastique,* or several moments towards the end of Tchaikovsky's *Nutcracker* are instances. I listen to entire pieces with pleasure, but during those fleeting moments of genius I experience deep emotion, a kind of ecstasy. It may be the melody or the timbre or the particular sound of a cello or oboe; it's not always the same. There is that occasional grace beyond the reach of art which provides virtual perfection in the realm of music, and I respond to it with thanksgiving.

## *At Symphony*

Halfway through the movement's desert fare
One passage bloomed in sudden beauty, rare
And perfect in the blend the artist's care
Achieved in rhythm, timbre, range, and air.

That moment made the whole worthwhile, so fair
In essence that my spirit soared in prayer,
Borne up by strong emotion, unaware
Of all but stunning sounds beyond compare.

## *Relationships*

Our lives are a network
Of crisscrossing lines.
We swing in our orbits
Attracting
Repelling
Like planets in space.

We wheel in our courses
As gravities pull,
Sustained every moment
Through pulling
And pushing
While we hurtle on.

We're interdependent,
Like the moon and the sun.
We balance each other
By giving
And taking
Each day we're alive.

## *Gift of God*

I reveled in *Giovanni*
I hummed *The Magic Flute*
I wept the matchless *Requiem*
Till spellbound, I sat mute.

I wondered at each passage,
Absorbed in harmony,
I trembled at the power
Of sounds that ravished me.

God whispered in the softness,
God murmured in each swell—
I thrilled to truth and beauty,
And rejoiced in them to dwell.

>  (Amadeus means "Love of God" or "Gift of God.")

## Or I Die

The violet at the window gropes for light,
Its purple head peeps out from indoor night.
If, when watered, in apparent spite
I turn the pot half round, within the sight
Of one sun's pass, or two, the plant will fight
To face its source of warmth, of life and might.
The violet at the window must have light.

## *Family Treasures*

I like the feel of old but useful things . . .
The kitchen table which the children scarred,
The walnut chest restored though somewhat marred,
The old oak rockers where we sit like kings
To view our wedding plate while my soul sings,
The antique bedroom set we share at rest,
The ancient cherry chair . . . these all attest
To ease of life. Each quiet comfort brings.
I like to hold your hand, to view your face,
To reminisce in fondness, touch your hair,
To talk or show my love through an embrace
That says (I hope) you are to me most fair.
How fitting, then, while we grow old apace
We have the old familiar things to share.

## *Memories*

I write my sorrows in the sand
Or surface of a lake;
They slowly vanish from my sight
And hardly leave an ache.

I carve my joys in adamant
In letters bright and tall,
Encouraged then through memory's voice
To face what may befall.

## *Drouth*

Tendance without love
   Or service without care
Is like clouds without rain
   Or croplands brown and bare.

## *Retirement*

One rocks and stares and twists about,
All hope long since abandoned:
Rocking, sleeping, racked with doubt,
He wears each threadbare minute out.

Another packs each day so tight
He scarce has room to breathe in:
Coming, going, eyes alight,
He crowds the clock from dawn 'til night.

## *Two at Eighty*

Arthritic fingers could not press
The strings and, brokenhearted, John
Threw down the mandolin he'd hugged,
Squeezed out a tear despite a will
To bear the burden of his years.

The wrinkles and the laugh lines merged
To form her radiant face, two eyes
That witnessed to a peace within
Despite the thousand creases pain
And sorrow long had deeply etched.

## *John Michener*

The glow above the city slowly dimmed
As panoramic lights ceased one by one.
The heavens darkened as the city went
To sleep, extinguishing in turn the rays
That pierced the night. I thought of John, whose light
Shone clear for ninety years in selfless acts
Of love. He worked for others, serving them
In Meeting and without. He taught, he helped
His fellows gain much needed funds, he worked
For peace and justice, truth and faith. His loss
Meant deeper shadows when the light went out.

## *Dialogue*

Soul: A temple is a splendid place
      To serve God in this earthly race.
      Despite the limits you impose
      I'm thankful for this calm repose.

Body: My limbs are lithe, my senses keen
      Because you deign to live within.
      I'm glad to host a gracious guest
      And offer occupance and rest.

Soul: Your chambers are so clean and neat
      I clap my hands and stamp my feet.
      I flourish in this regal space
      A cut above the commonplace.

Body: My sacred pledge to God I gave
      To offer all as bonded slave
      That spirit might, within these walls
      Respond to God's directive calls.

Soul: I add my voice to yours and give
      Fair notice that I mean to live
      Serenely, choosing not to roam,
      While tenant in this pleasant home.

Body: I too rejoice in harmony.
      As perfect partners we shall be
      The image of our Lord above
      And teach all creatures of his love.

## Active Aging

"He never misses Meals on Wheels,"
The supervisor said. "Through rain
And snow, he's on the go. He feels
The homebound need such care and pain."

"Indeed, I know a man who tends
His neighbor's yard (a wheelchair case),
Who aids his helpless friend with ends
As free of guile as childhood's face."

"Oh, sure," the supervisor said,
"I know other folks like that.
One oldster tutors kids instead
Of idly rocking in his flat.

"Another reads to blind folks, writes
Their letters, helps them shop. Why, one
Man coaches ghetto kids, ignites
Their courage, helps them reach the sun."

"Such things seem right to me," agreed
The guest. "A cup of water in
Christ's name, a coat, a coin, or deed
Of kindness surely honor Him."

## *Wheels Within Wheels*

I contemplate the cycles
   That govern daily life—
The ends and the beginnings,
   The peace that follows strife.

I watch a storm to silence
   While braving wind and rain,
Then revel in the sunshine
   That floods the earth again.

Each dawn gives way to evening
   And life succumbs to death;
My son becomes a father
   While I draw shorter breath.

The seeds of spring grow golden
   And harvest grains roll in;
The summer's sun arcs lower,
   Ere winter's snows begin.

I pause in meditation
   On Mystery and Power
Revealed in constant motion
   And worship in that hour.

## *Life Runs Out*

Life runs out like sifting grain:
It spots the earth like golden rain,
Pouring in a steady stream
From some lower grainbox seam.

Children heedless go their way
Happy in their careless play,
Sustained each day with love and care
They take for granted will be there.

Youths move further to the west,
Restless in their endless quest
For sense and meaning, seeking well,
Though dazzled by the moment's spell.

Men and women play their parts,
Act their roles, in fits and starts,
Pausing seldom mid-career
To ask of whither—there? or here?

Even age moves steady on
Night by night, and dawn by dawn,
Too frail to struggle much, or sing,
Condemned instead to limbo's ring.

Life runs out like running grain:
It seeds the earth in golden rain,
Dropping, falling to the plain
Unnoticed, till the box is drained.

## *Ending Is Beginning*

The phoenix rises from its funeral pyre
    Newborn from out the ashes of the dead
    Exactly as each New Year springs to life
From out the embers of a twelvemonth fire.

Old Winter storms his way across the plains
    Until young Spring unseats him from his mount,
    But Summer soon displaces Spring, till Fall
Breaks ailing Summer's grip on sagging reins.

Commencement is a sentimental end
    As well as a beginning; caps and gowns
    Preserve a storied past while sparkling eyes
Anticipate fresh epics to be penned.

Each year brings sorrow through unwelcome death
    As faithful friends fall one by one to rest.
    Yet surely just beyond the veil is birth,
New life to spirits freed at last from breath.

(The phoenix is a legendary bird which lived five hundred years, burned itself to ashes on a pyre, and rose a chick to live another five hundred years. It thus became a symbol for immortality or deathlessness.)

## *Heartbeat*

The metronome within keeps pace
With pendulums and wheels, with clocks
That daily stalk their prey, that chase
Their quarry in life's steady race.

The moments stalk each living thing
(All blossoms wither while time creeps)
As sundials, watches, poised to spring
Approach each victim with their sting.

## *Betrayal*

The silent snow lies soft and smooth,
Erasing scars on fence and field.
All seems so peaceful, so at rest.
Yet in the morning light appear
The tracks of rabbit, fox, and quail
In patterns interlaced.

I add my imprint to the scene
And pensive ask of hunted and
The hunt . . . "How can these co-exist?
How can weak ones live, betrayed
By footprints in the snow?"

A composing stick is a tool, a flat adjustable holder for movable type. The old-fashioned typesetter filled the composing stick with the letters and spacers which made up lines of type, the sentences that would appear as a finished product in a book or newspaper. The typesetter worked all day, filling the stick until his composition was done.

## *Composing Stick*

Life is composed
    Piece by piece
        Day by day
Of trifling little acts
With here and there a main event.

Take
  A birth
    A desk
      A cap and gown
        A printing press
          A wedding cake
            A child or two
              An anniversary plate
            A death
And fit in all the sleeps,
    The breakfasts, lunches, dinners, trips,
      The clothes and chores and colds,
Until these fully cram the stick,
The composition done.